TINY
TITANS

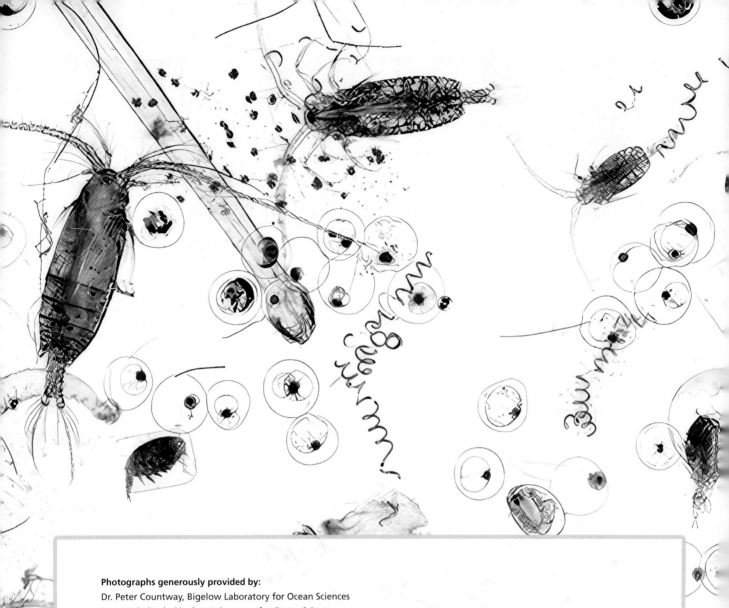

Photographs generously provided by:
Dr. Peter Countway, Bigelow Laboratory for Ocean Sciences
Laura Lubelczyk, Bigelow Laboratory for Ocean Sciences
Bigelow Laboratory for Ocean Sciences
Dr. Nick Record, Bigelow Laboratory for Ocean Sciences
Friends of Casco Bay
and Anna Dibble

© David Liittschwager/Wikimedia Commons, 2-3; © NASA, 4-5, 22-23, 27; © Christian Sardet, 6-7, 8, 15, 28, 38, 39; © Dr. Peter Countway, Bigelow Laboratory for Ocean Sciences, 10, 12, 14, 17, 35; © Laura Lubelczyk, Bigelow Laboratory for Ocean Sciences, 13, 16, 39; © RugliG/Shutterstock, 18-19; © Chantal de Bruijne/Shutterstock, 20; © Bigelow Laboratory for Ocean Science, 21, 52; © Chisholm Lab/Wikimedia Commons, 24; © H2osol/Shutterstock, 29; © Hans Hillewaert/ Wikimedia Commons, 30; © Friends of Casco Bay, 30, 51; © RLS Photo/Shutterstock, 33; © Dr. Nick Record, Bigelow Laboratory for Ocean Sciences, 33; © divedog/Shutterstock, 34; © NOAA, 36; © Gina Lonati/Wikimedia Commons, 37; © Dan Hershman/Flickr, 40; © Paolo Gamba/Wikimedia Commons, 40; © Alice Wanwarameth/Shutterstock, 41; © Ihi/Shutterstock, 42; © Fabriguarni/Wikimedia Commons, 42; © Magnus Hagdorn/Flickr, 43; © Martin Prochazkacz/ Shutterstock, 44; © James Willamor/Flickr, 45; © USFWS - Pacific Region/Flickr, 46; © Daniel Di Palma/Wikimedia Commons, 48; © Dr. Jelena Godrijan, Bigelow Laboratory for Ocean Sciences, 53; © Anna Dibble, 54-55

TINY TITANS

The Big Story of Plankton

MARY M. CERULLO

TILBURY HOUSE PUBLISHERS

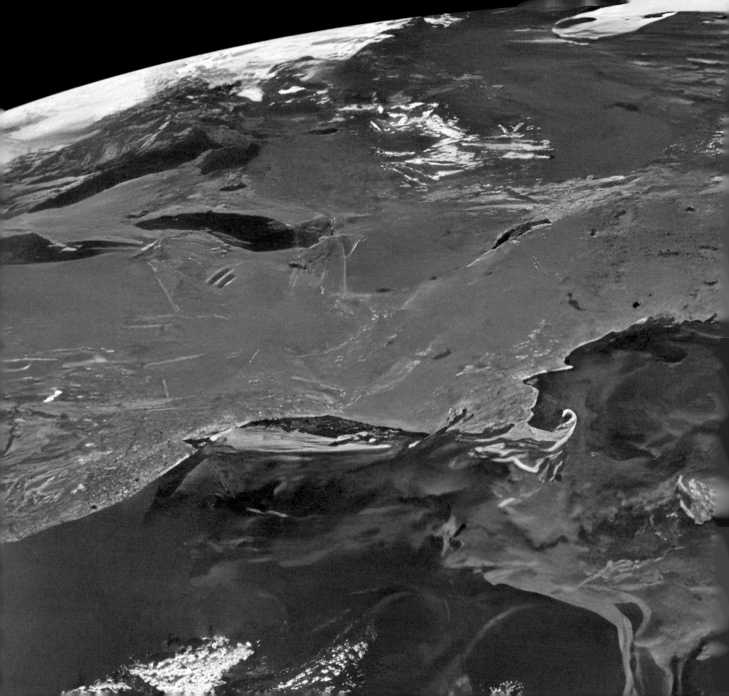

Wanderer. Nomad. Voyager.

Do those words make you think of an adventurer on a journey of exploration, danger, and excitement? Now imagine that you are that world traveler crossing a vast ocean. Except, you might be microscopic in size. How would you survive in the hungry ocean, surrounded by organisms that want to eat you? How would you escape predators, capture or make your food, and live long enough to contribute to another generation of your kind?

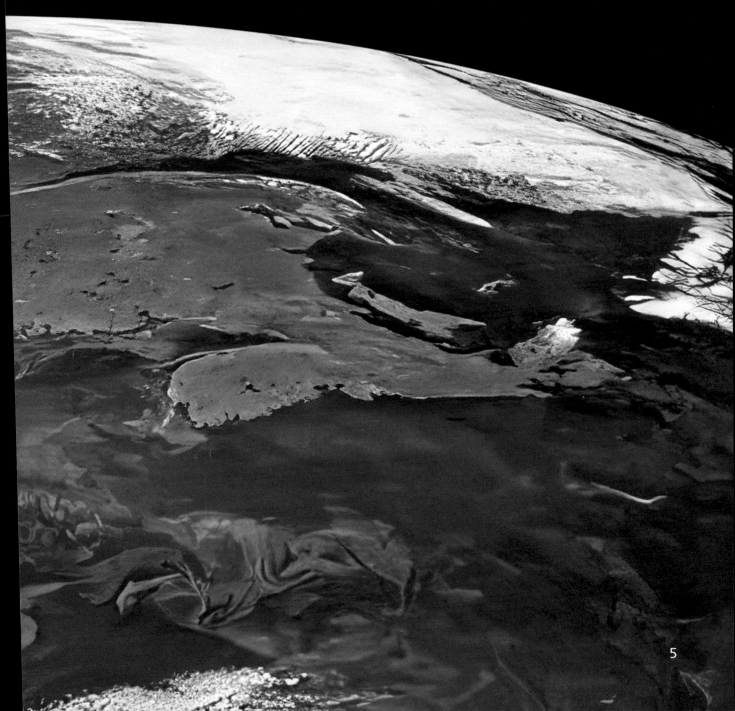

Scour the sunlit layers of the ocean

and you will meet many amazing characters that do all that and more. They also anchor the ocean **food web**, help slow climate change, and produce half the oxygen we breathe. They are *plankton*.

Plankton are named from the Greek word for "wanderer," because they drift on the water at the mercy of the waves, tides, and currents.

That is not to say these tiny creatures only float along wherever the waves take them. Many can move on their own, using whiplike tails or winged feet, to stay near the surface to soak up the sun or to dive into dark waters to avoid hungry predators.

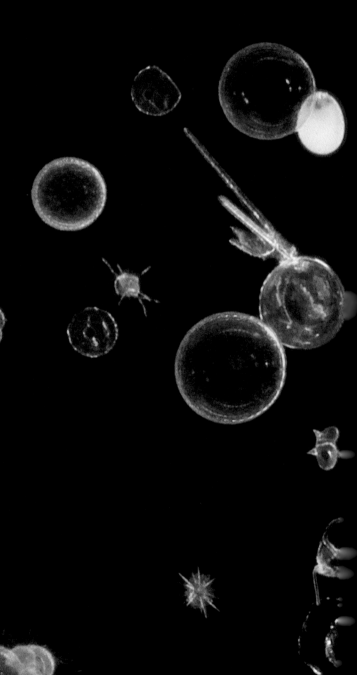

There are *phytoplankton*—drifting plants, including jewel-like **diatoms** and twirling **dinoflagellates**. And there are *zooplankton*—floating animals, including turbocharged **copepods**, armored **krill**, and much more.

Phytoplankton can capture energy from the sun and transform it into sugars and carbohydrates.

Zooplankton get their energy from capturing and eating phytoplankton and other zooplankton, and in turn make that energy available to larger animals.

Together, they make up the sea soup that feeds the rest of the ocean food web.

This isn't an image of outer space swirling with green planets and alien spaceships. It's inner space—our own microscopic ocean.

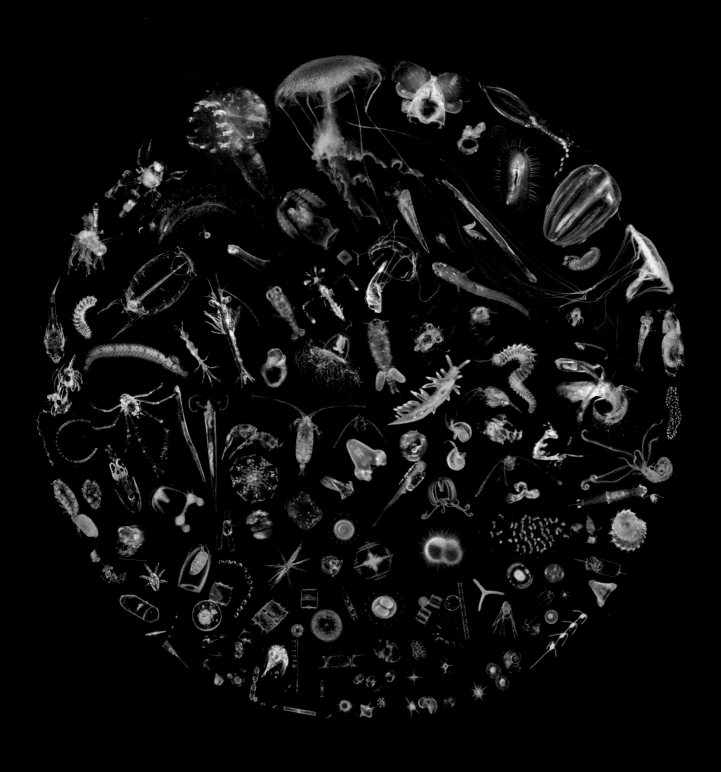

Another name for plankton:
Superheroes

Most plankton are tiny creatures that were nearly invisible to humans before microscopes were invented. Despite their small size, plankton display characteristics that could describe a cast of superheroes. Their powers include speed, endurance, adaptability, longevity, invisibility, and shape shifting.

And diversity. Dozens of extraordinary fictional characters populate comic books, movies, and television. Many *thousands* of real-life plankton species populate oceans, lakes, and even mudholes. Biologists can only guess how many kinds there are, because new ones are discovered all the time.

The extraordinary powers of superheroes are used for good, at least most of the time. Get ready to meet some of the leading plankton superheroes, as well as a few villains in the plankton universe.

There are legions of tiny plankton superheroes. There are more than 200 kinds of plankton just in this picture, but there are many, many more. Some are smaller than the period at the end of a sentence. Others are too big to fit on this page. You will meet many of these characters in this book and learn why we call them Tiny Titans!

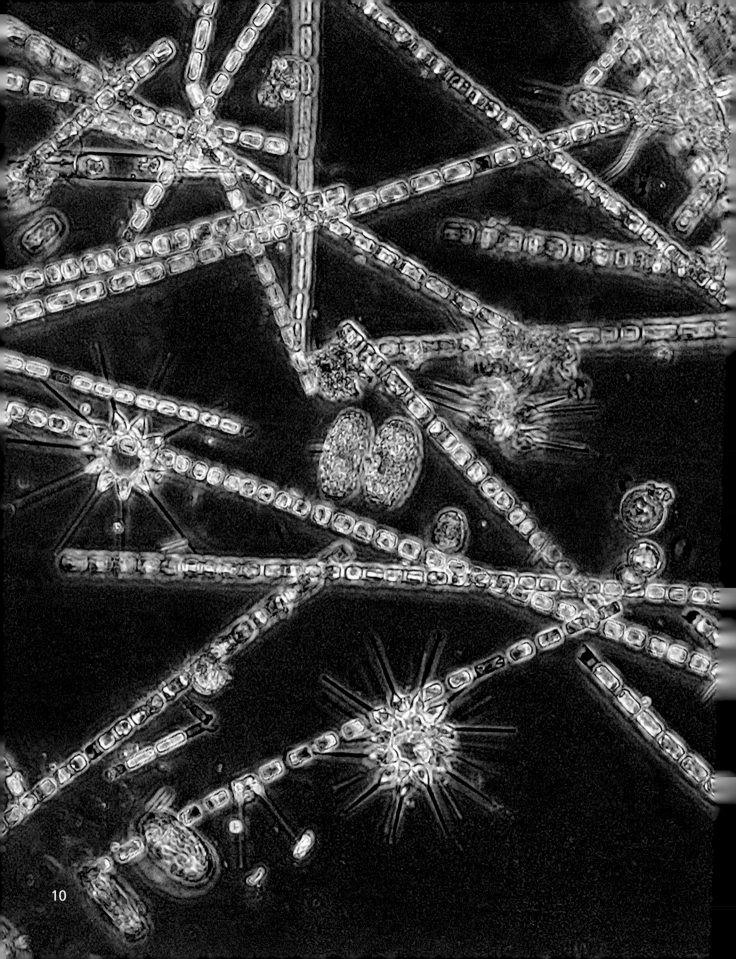

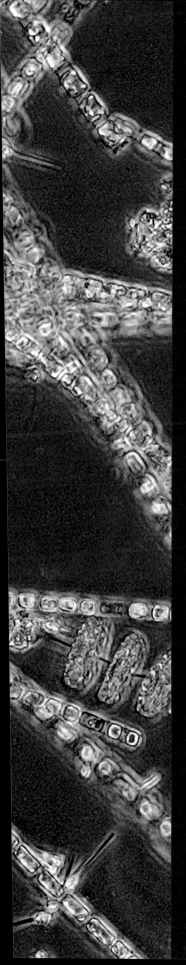

Phytos forever!

Phytoplankton provide oxygen for humans and food for sea life

Like plants on land, phytoplankton and other marine plants possess a chemical called **chlorophyll** that changes sunlight into sugars and other carbohydrates, ingredients you might find on the nutrition labels of cereal boxes and most of the foods we eat.

This chemical reaction, called **photosynthesis**, takes just a hundred-millionth of a minute to complete. It also makes much of the oxygen that humans and other animals need to breathe.

These microscopic plants (also called *microalgae*) don't look like the plants on land. They have no roots, stems, or leaves. Instead they resemble bristly balls, tiny harpoons, links on a bracelet, spaceships, and other shapes that defy description.

Diatoms, dinoflagellates, and coccolithophores are the big three of phytoplankton.

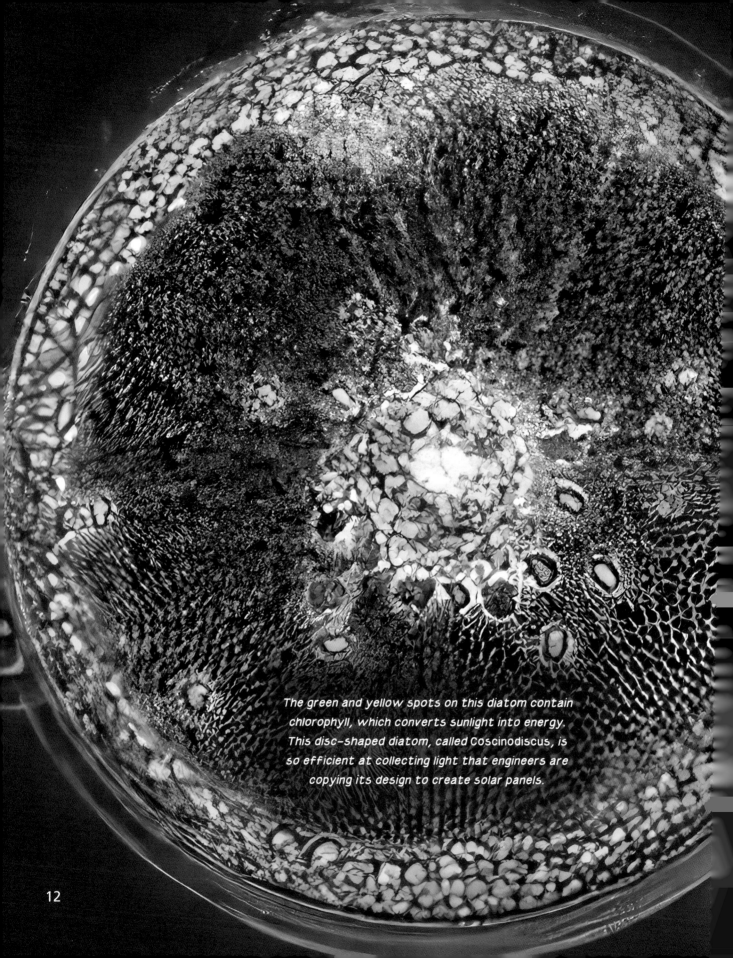

The green and yellow spots on this diatom contain chlorophyll, which converts sunlight into energy. This disc-shaped diatom, called Coscinodiscus, is so efficient at collecting light that engineers are copying its design to create solar panels.

Diatoms

Solar-powered phytofactories produce
what sea creatures want and humans need

A *diatom* is a plant that lives inside a glass greenhouse of its own creation. Diatoms build their clear shells from silica, a mineral dissolved in seawater. Silica is the same material that is used to make the windows of our home, drinking glasses in our cupboards, and even our cell phones!

Diatoms get their name from the Greek word *diatomos*, which means "cut in two." That's because they reproduce by dividing in two. Then each diatom divides again and again. Because a diatom can divide every 18 to 36 hours, one becomes many within a few days. In fact, diatoms are among the most abundant phytoplankton in the ocean. And that is a lucky thing, because:

Diatoms nourish the ocean food web. Even though their glass houses make their shells slightly heavier than seawater, they float thanks to oil they store as extra food. Oil makes diatoms a nourishing meal for organisms farther up the food chain.

Diatoms help us breathe. As a byproduct of photosynthesis, diatoms generate 20 to 50 percent of the oxygen produced on the planet each year!

These diatoms, called Thalassiosira, *bloom in early spring, providing an important source of food for newly hatched fish looking for their first meal.*

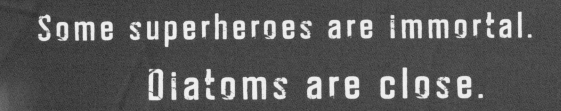

Some superheroes are immortal.
Diatoms are close.

These tough little plants can survive almost anywhere there is light, water, and **nutrients**, even in mud. One curious scientist came upon some diatoms that had dried out on a piece of paper in 1834. Much to his surprise, when he immersed them in water, they revived and began to swim around, nearly 200 years later!

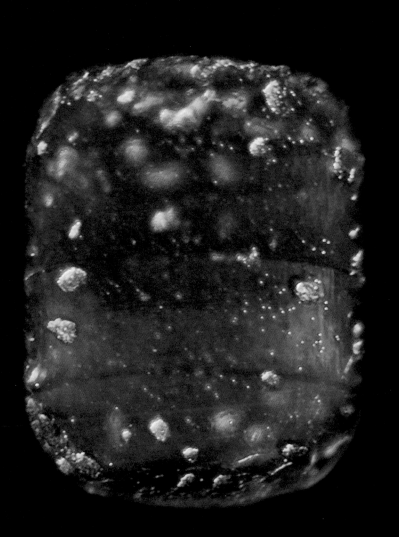

Diatoms vary in size, shape, and habit. Some
are loners and others link together in long
chains to keep them afloat near the surface.

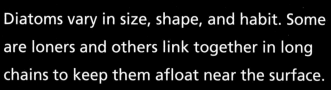

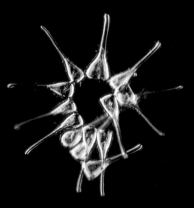

The chemical
makeup of a diatom's shell
is almost the same as the gemstone
opal. Maybe that's why these colorful
diatoms are often called the "jewels of the sea."

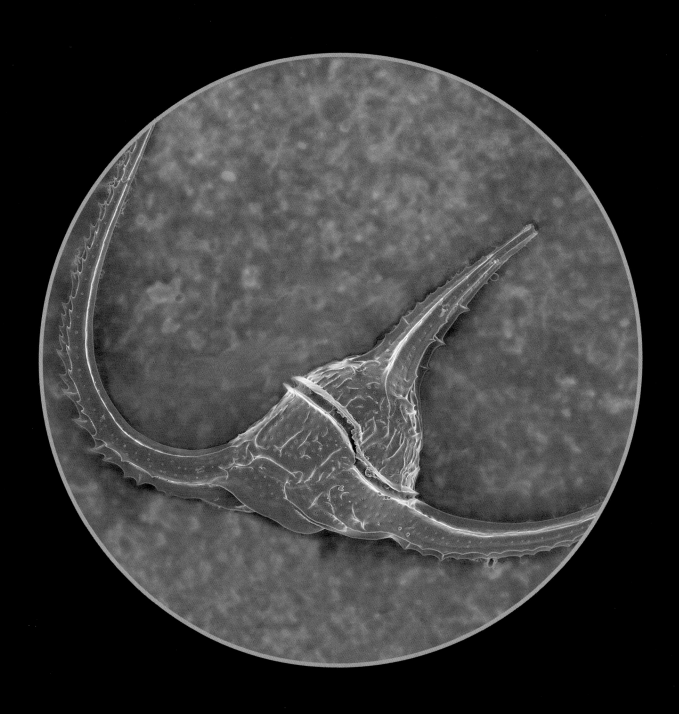

Dinoflagellates are phytoplankton with attitude. They do more than just drift on the currents. They can flex their flagella to move under their own power.

Dinoflagellates

Whirling whips that whisk through the ocean

Most phytoplankton merely drift along with the waves and currents. *Dinoflagellates*, though, can move under their own power. That is because they have two twitching tails that act as built-in propellers.

The name *dinoflagellate* comes from Latin: dinos means "whirling" and flagella means "whips." One tail, or flagellum, runs down the length of the cell's body, and the other encircles its middle like a belt. Together, the two tails propel dinoflagellates through the water like twirling ballerinas.

Even with two tails, dinoflagellates aren't great swimmers. Dinoflagellates prefer calm water where they can stay near the surface to get the sunlight they need to photosynthesize. But their whiplike tails enable them to dive into slightly deeper water when they need to find fresh patches of nutrients.

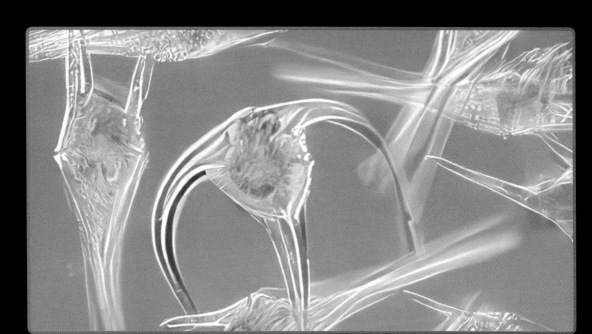

The Blue Flash

On the coast of Australia, you might find yourself watching the tide come in on a moonless night. The water crashes against the rocks and, suddenly, flashes of light explode in blue-green splendor. You have just witnessed one of the greatest superpowers in the ocean: **bioluminescence**.

Millions of sparkling dinoflagellates put on an underwater light show in Jervis Bay, Australia. When disturbed, the "dinos" emit a sudden flash of light, gone in a tenth of a second.

Bioluminescence is the production of light by a living creature through a chemical reaction. Some call it "cold fire," because only a small amount of the energy is released as heat.

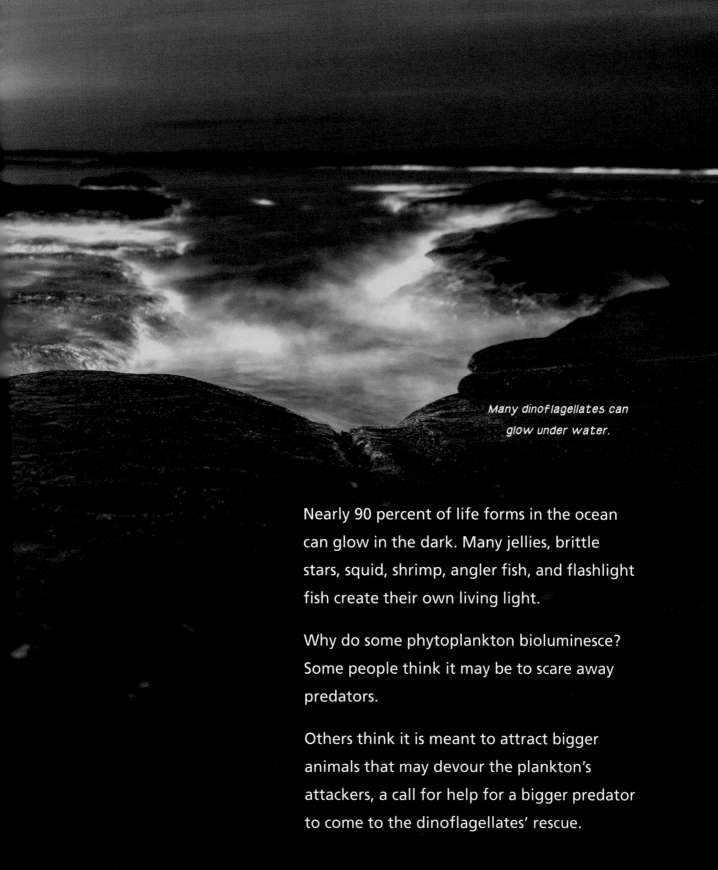

Many dinoflagellates can glow under water.

Nearly 90 percent of life forms in the ocean can glow in the dark. Many jellies, brittle stars, squid, shrimp, angler fish, and flashlight fish create their own living light.

Why do some phytoplankton bioluminesce? Some people think it may be to scare away predators.

Others think it is meant to attract bigger animals that may devour the plankton's attackers, a call for help for a bigger predator to come to the dinoflagellates' rescue.

Coccolithophores
Warriors in white armor

Astronauts circling the Earth have sometimes been surprised to see areas of the ocean's surface turn a milky white. Those astronauts were looking down at a bloom of billions of **coccolithophores**. Coccolithophores are encased in armored plates shaped like the round shields of ancient gladiators. Their white shells are made of calcium carbonate, the same material found in the shells of clams and skeletons of corals.

Scientists need their strongest microscopes to see coccolithophores. They use an electron microscope that can magnify an object up to 1,000,000 times. Yet these tiny phytoplankton can build mountains.

Sculptor Julie Crane made it easy to admire a coccolithophore, which normally can only be seen if you have a powerful electron microscope.

After coccolithophores die, they sink to the bottom of the sea. Their shells pile up, layer upon layer, until they become compressed into a rock called limestone. Eventually, after millions of years, the limestone is pushed above the ocean surface by the same movements of the Earth's crust that form mountain ranges. On the White Cliffs of Dover in England, you can walk on the skeletons of these microscopic algae.

Coccolithophores build their own suits of protective armor. Their overlapping plates, called liths, are made of calcium carbonate, the same material that clams and oysters extract from seawater to build their shells. The White Cliffs of Dover are made of layers of prehistoric coccolithophores.

Coccolithophore blooms—huge hordes of these tiny phytoplankton—reflect nearly all the sunlight that hits them back into space. In this way, coccolithophores help slow climate change—at least for a while. By reflecting light back into space, less heat is absorbed by the ocean and atmosphere to warm the planet.

You might do something similar yourself when you decide to wear a white shirt on a hot, sunny day, rather than a dark top that would absorb more heat.

Scientists measure how much light is reflected back from the surfaces of glaciers, clouds, or snow-capped mountains. This is called **albedo**.

Sometimes masses of coccolithophores
can be seen from outer space.

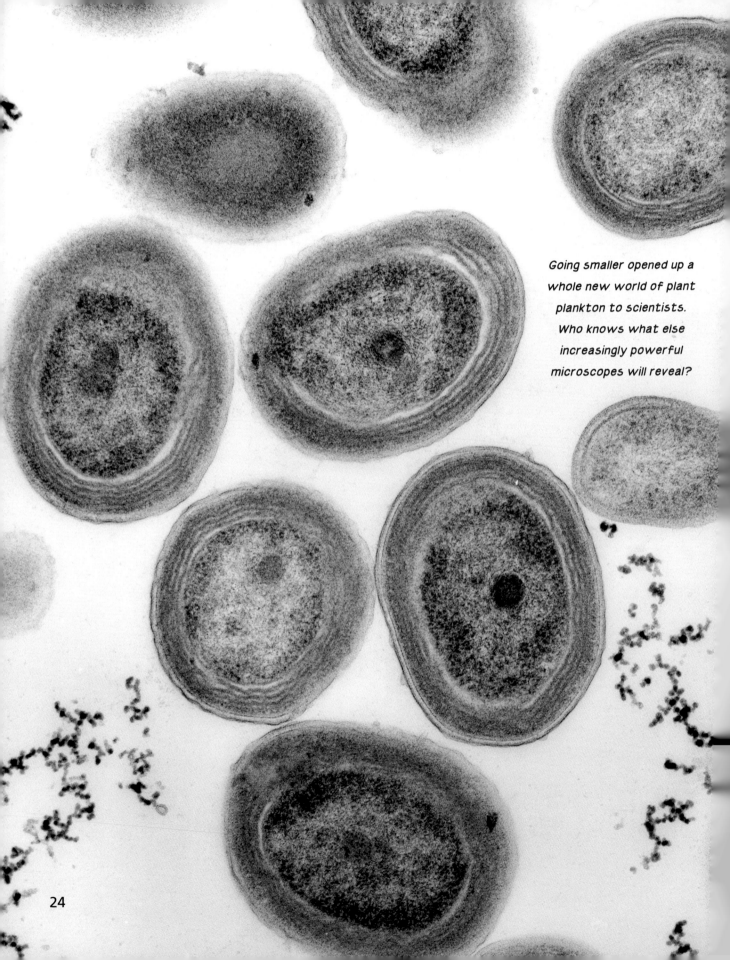

Going smaller opened up a whole new world of plant plankton to scientists. Who knows what else increasingly powerful microscopes will reveal?

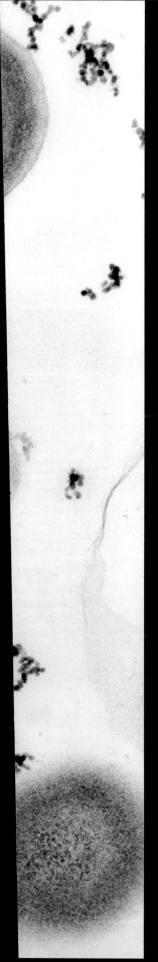

Teeny tiny nanoplankton live in an alternate universe

As numerous as diatoms, dinoflagellates, and coccolithophores are, they are a drop in the bucket compared with the alternative universe that only the most powerful microscopes can reveal. What researchers once thought were specks of dust in their microscopes are actually amazingly small phytoplankton.

As microscopes improved, researchers discovered a whole new world of tiny life forms. We are surrounded by the smallest but most numerous phytoplankton of all: nanophytoplankton and even smaller **picoplankton**. Scientists believe there are more creatures of this size in the ocean than all other plankton combined.

They live alongside other incredibly tiny creatures—bacteria, protists, viruses, and even giant viruses called *giruses* (fortunately, giruses don't infect humans!).

These extraordinarily tiny creatures are good for the ocean. **Nanoplankton** feed a large number of zooplankton. Some even appear to tame the toxicity o some of the poisonous phytoplankton antiheroes you are about to meet.

Phytoplankton Antiheroes
Red Tides: When phytoplankton go BAD

On land, the word "bloom" might describe multicolored tulips or the pink blossoms of flowering cherry trees. In the ocean, you might see red.

Nutrients stirred up from deep water or from fertilizers and sewage washed off the land can make billions of phytoplankton bloom. Some of these blooms are harmless.

Others are dangerous. When toxic blooms occur, people call them red tides, because sometimes the water turns the color of blood. (Other times, the water may look yellow, brown, or green.) Scientists call these outbreaks **harmful algal blooms**. There are thousands of different kinds of phytoplankton, but only about 200 species form harmful algal blooms.

Shellfish, such as clams and oysters, or small fish, such as herring or baby cod, may eat infected phytoplankton. They are not usually harmed themselves, but they concentrate the toxins in their tissues and pass them along to whatever animal is unlucky enough to eat them. Animals higher up the food chain, such as salmon, pelicans, dolphins, manatees, whales, and humans may get sick and even die.

Pick your poison.

Toxic microalgae affect their victims in different ways:

Paralytic shellfish poisoning causes a person to go numb and have difficulty breathing. In extreme cases, people have died from eating contaminated clams, mussels, and oysters.

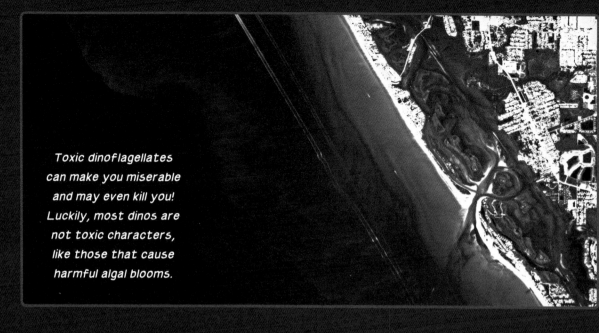

Toxic dinoflagellates can make you miserable and may even kill you! Luckily, most dinos are not toxic characters, like those that cause harmful algal blooms.

Amnesiac shellfish poisoning can cause people to lose their memory. Some victims can't even remember their own names. Alarmingly, some people get sick just by breathing in air around where these dinoflagellates are present.

Diarrhetic shellfish poisoning doesn't kill you. One victim who suffered bouts of vomiting, stomach pain, and diarrhea said, "It just makes you wish you were dead."

Nothing ruins a tropical vacation like getting *ciguatera poisoning*. Small, plant-eating coral reef fish nibble on toxic dinoflagellates called *ciguatera*. The fish are eaten by larger predators, such as barracuda, groupers, and moray eels. Unfortunately, diners can't tell whether or not a fish is tainted with ciguatera poison. It looks, smells, and tastes the same as a harmless fish. Cooking doesn't destroy the toxin.

The first signs are similar to those of diarrhetic shellfish poisoning. Weird, long-lasting effects may follow, including hiccups, itching, and acne. Some victims complain that when they touch something cold, it feels hot, and hot feels cold. It may take years to recover completely.

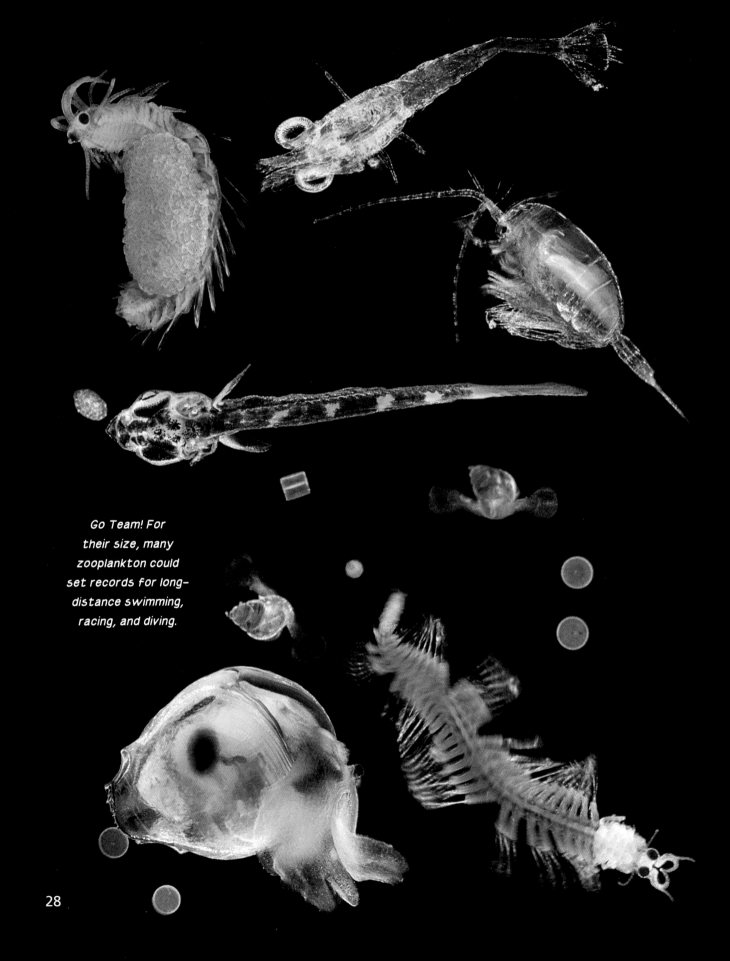

Go Team! For their size, many zooplankton could set records for long-distance swimming, racing, and diving.

Zooplankton Arise!

Zooplankton can dive to the deep ocean, change their form, and be all but invisible.

Some zooplankton spend over 80 percent of their time moving under their own power—mostly up and down. They may take daily journeys from the surface to the depths of the sea, often moving hundreds of feet, sometimes even thousands of feet. The change in temperature is like going from Brazil to Iceland in one night.

Zooplankton move down as the daylight increases, possibly to escape the many predators that crowd the surface. At night, when predators can't see them, they rise to the water's surface to feed on phytoplankton. Like other sea creatures that venture into the deep, dark ocean, many zooplankton, such as krill, can flash their living lights. Some copepods squirt glowing bioluminescent clouds from their butts as they zip past startled predators.

Zooplankton are much larger than phytoplankton. Many are large enough to be seen with an ordinary magnifying lens. That includes the eggs of sea animals, their newly hatched offspring, many small creatures, and even some big ones.

There are even giant zooplankton, like the Portuguese man-of-war. Its air-filled balloon enables it to float as much as six inches above the water's surface. Its stinging tentacles can trail 30 feet or more behind it.

Floating at the sunlit ocean surface makes this zooplankton baby an easy meal for hungry hunters.

Some zooplankton are transformers, too

Most sea creatures start life as zooplankton. In the ocean, it's common for newly hatched fish, crabs, lobsters, barnacles, snails, clams, and sea stars to look more like space aliens than like their parents.

In their **larval** stages, they float at the ocean's surface. This phase may last a few hours or several months. They are only temporary plankton. Scientists call them *meroplankton*. Eventually they grow into miniature versions of their adult selves. They change into bottom-dwelling crabs, lobsters, worms, or sea stars. Or they may turn into strong swimmers like cod and herring.

Some zooplankton never change. Those zooplankton spend their entire lives drifting with the currents. They are called permanent plankton—or, in the language of science, *holoplankton*.

While temporary plankton tend to live near the coast, permanent plankton often live in the open ocean, where landlubbers would rarely encounter them. That may be why many of us may not know about permanent zooplankton such as copepods, krill, sea butterflies, salps, and comb jellies.

Even after it transforms into a bottom-hugging lobster, its chances of survival are grim. This one has already lost one of its defensive claws. With luck, it might live long enough to grow a new one.

For some zooplankton, invisibility is their superpower

Some permanent zooplankton seem to disappear in the water. It may be because these gelatinous zooplankton are over 95 percent water.

You might be tempted to gently poke a gelatinous animal to see if it feels like Jell-O, but it could fall apart at your touch.

A comb jelly is one such gelatinous sea creature. A bioluminescent comb jelly sports eight rows of twinkling, colored lights. It gets its name from the eight rows of tiny hairs arranged like the teeth on a comb. The hairs beat in unison to propel it through the water, like a team of rowers pulling on the oars of a racing boat.

Another gooey animal is the **salp**, which floats almost
invisibly through the ocean depths. Eight bands of muscles
encircle its barrel-shaped body. When it squeezes its muscles, the salp
shoots forward in a spiral motion. It shovels in food as it rolls along.

Salps often live together in colonies of 500 individuals or more. They can
form a chain as long as a school bus. Yet salps are so delicate that a sweep
of a diver's hand through the water a foot away could tear them to pieces.

Meet the superheroes of the zooplankton world.

Copepods, krill, and sea butterflies are the big three of zooplankton.

Their vast numbers nourish almost all the other animals in the ocean.

Copepods
Submarine speed demons

Tiny cousins to lobsters and crabs, *copepods* are one-eyed creatures with two antennae as long as their whole body. A copepod in search of a meal stretches out its antennae like radar, waiting for signals from the sea. If it senses danger, it slaps them against its body and darts away. It can propel itself up to 500 times its body length in less than a second. The effect is like being shot from a cannon.

How fast is a copepod?

No one gets more excited about copepods than Cabell Davis, a biologist at Woods Hole Oceanographic Institution. He once wondered, "If a cheetah, the fastest animal on land, and a copepod, the fastest animal in the ocean, held a race, who would win?"

He calculated that if a cheetah and a copepod were the same size, a cheetah running at 70 miles per hour would compare to a copepod moving at 2,000 miles per hour!

For such tiny animals, one-eyed copepods sure get up, down, and around. They rise to the surface at night and dive to deeper, darker depths at dawn. They are found in every corner of the world's oceans.

Blue whales can weigh more
than 165 tons and grow
more than 110 feet long.

KRILL
The pink swarm

What sea creatures can dive a half mile from the ocean's surface to the deep sea and back again in a single day, blink like fireflies in an underwater sky, and are no bigger than your thumb? Krill!

Krill look a lot like their cousins: shrimp, crayfish, and crabs. Like other crustaceans, krill have to molt or shed their shells to grow larger ones. If food is scarce, krill can actually shrink in size to conserve energy.

Their shells are dotted with small red spots. In Antarctica, krill gather close to the ocean's surface in such huge groups, called swarms, that their shells sometimes turn the water pink.

There are so many krill that the largest animals in the world—blue whales—can survive on a steady diet of these tiny crustaceans. One scientist estimated that a blue whale eats about 6,000 pounds (2,700 kg) of krill each day. In fact, the word *krill* in Norwegian means whale food. When Norwegian whale hunters spotted schools of these crusty creatures, they knew they had found the whales' feeding grounds.

A constellation of krill

Krill can light up the ocean, thanks to tiny light organs. Scientists named them *euphausiids*, the Greek term for "shining brightly." Why they should glow in the dark is a mystery to scientists, but they think that the source of their bioluminescence may come from the diatoms they devour.

Krill can see quite well. They have compound eyes, like insect eyes, so they can see both up and down at the same time. It's a great way to watch for predators and prey at the same time!

37

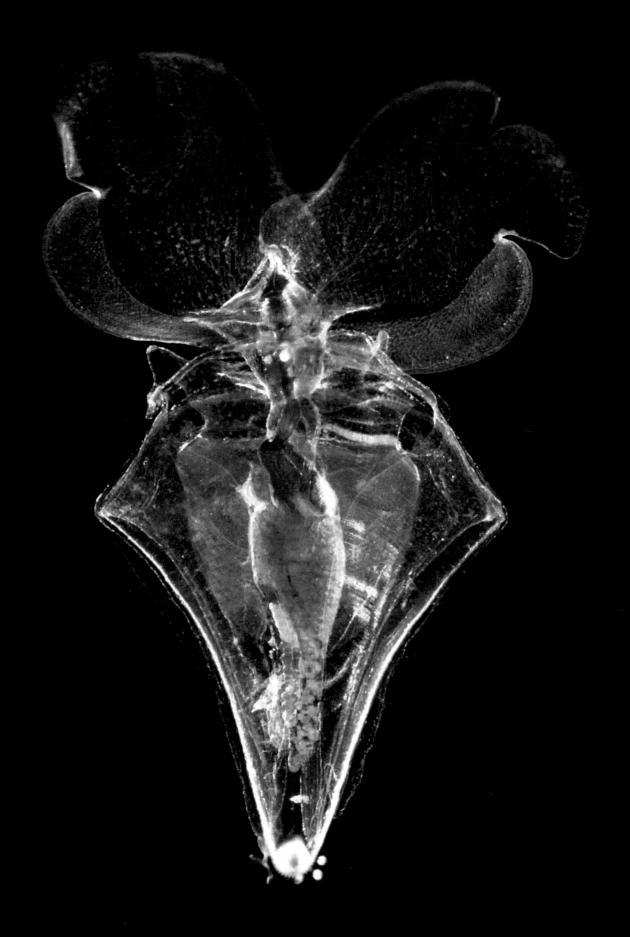

Pteropods
Winged wonders

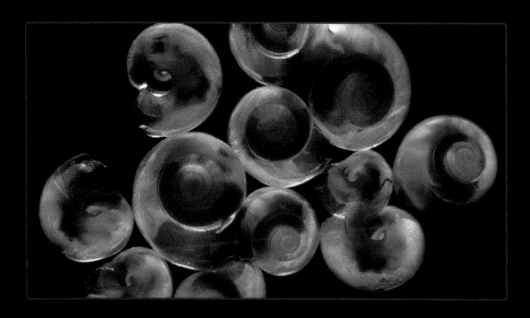

Wispy sea butterflies are also called **pteropods**, which means "wing-footed." These creatures flap through the water on tiny wings that are extensions of their feet.

They are mollusks, so they have shells like snails and clams. But their shells are so paper thin that you can see right through them.

Sea butterflies: so lovely—until they eat

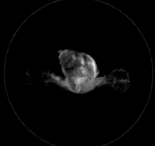

Pteropods look delicate as they flit through the ocean, but they don't look so appealing when you watch how they eat. Sea butterflies secrete a sticky mucous web to snare passing plankton and the tiny organic particles that scientists call "marine snow." That picturesque term actually describes flakes of decaying sea creatures, shed skin, poop, mucous, and other tasty tidbits that drift down toward the ocean floor.

Zooplankton Rogues
Tentacled titans

Is it a nightmare or real life? A creature with no head, spine, or heart suddenly ambushes you as you are swimming in the ocean. A curtain of shimmering, twitching tentacles blocks your path. The tentacles are covered with coiled stinging cells, called *nematocysts*. They shoot out like harpoons when they

touch something edible, like YOU! The tentacles pull you into an opening under its umbrella, which is the closest thing it has to a mouth.

Luckily, you back up fast enough to avoid a collision with a lion's mane jellyfish. This jelly looks to be almost three feet across, and its tentacles may be up to 60 feet long.

"How does this gigantic creature qualify as plankton?" you may ask. Whatever their size, most sea jellies (which is what scientists call jellyfish) are zooplankton that are moved by the wind and the waves.

Jellies are cousins of sea anemones and corals, which also have nematocysts. There are many different kinds of jellies, some as small as a pea and others up to seven feet wide. Some, such as moon jellies, leave no impression on humans at all, while others can inflict painful welts. But beware! Even a dead jelly can sting, because its nematocysts are released if touched.

There are zooplankton you don't want to bump into!

Beware the sea wasp

The most dangerous jelly of them all is the sea wasp of Australia. In the ocean around Queensland, Australia, more swimmers have been killed by sea wasps in the past 100 years than by great white sharks.

A sea wasp the size of a grapefruit has enough venom to kill 60 adults. It does not sting a human on purpose, small comfort to the swimmer who blunders into its tentacles. Without medical help, the victim could be dead within minutes. Safety nets are strung across many swimming beaches in Australia to keep out sea wasps. Lifeguards stockpile medicine to treat victims quickly.

Sea turtles love to eat jellies. Their scaly head and a special lining in their throat protect them from the sting of the sea wasp.

Why Do Plankton Matter?

It sometimes seems that only the "bad" plankton—toxic algal blooms and venomous jellies—grab the headlines, while the good that plankton do for the world is all but ignored. Some of those benefits are worth repeating:

Plankton are the food basket of the sea

Phytoplankton and zooplankton feed the ocean food web. Nearly everything in the ocean depends on them, directly or indirectly. What a responsibility!

Phytoplankton are the lungs of our planet

Phytoplankton help us to breathe. Every other breath we take is thanks to phytoplankton.

Plankton slow climate change

The earth is getting warmer, mainly as a result of burning coal, oil, and gas, which add carbon dioxide and other heat-trapping gases to Earth's atmosphere. We are already witnessing the impact of climate change.

Phytoplankton use three *billion* tons of carbon dioxide annually. Through photosynthesis, phytoplankton break apart carbon dioxide into carbon and oxygen. Plankton capture "unwanted" excess carbon and take it out of

circulation, helping to slow climate change. Up to half the carbon absorbed by the ocean is carried into the deep ocean by plankton.

Many carbon atoms are taken up in the shells of sea creatures such as coccolithophores. When they die, their shells may sink to the bottom of the ocean, where the carbon they contain can't re-enter the atmosphere as a greenhouse gas. Even the tiniest phytoplankton—nanoplankton—capture large amounts of carbon that would otherwise be released as carbon dioxide.

Zooplankton also perform an important service that helps slow global warming. They poop! Zooplankton eat phytoplankton, digest them, and turn them into waste products called fecal pellets. Scientists have taken to calling them **zoop poop**. These pellets contain carbon.

Many of these fecal pellets are heavy enough to sink all the way to the ocean floor, thousands of feet below. Zooplankton such as salps make big pellets that sink quickly. Salp pellets can sink 3,000 feet in a day! Some of that carbon may remain at the bottom of the sea for thousands of years.

Mother whales go to warm waters to give birth, but to feed their newborn calves, they head to cold seas. There they find a feast of plankton that nourishes the rest of the ocean food web.

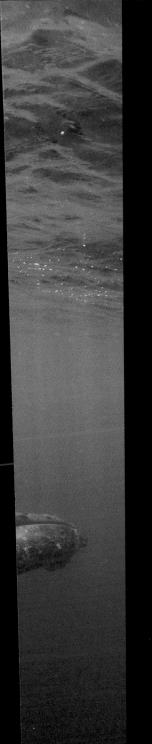

Plankton color the ocean

Poets describe the ocean as azure, aquamarine, cerulean, and other shades of blue, but the ocean's true color depends on where you are—and what is floating in the water. In colder climates, the water looks green, thanks to a salty mix of phytoplankton, zooplankton, and nutrients, the chemicals that plants and animals need to grow. Because of this thick broth of sea creatures, living and dead, you might only be able to see as far as the end of your fingertips when you dive into cold ocean waters.

If you were to go diving in the tropical ocean, the water would be so clear that you would be able to see a hundred feet around you in any direction. Where there is hardly any plankton—and less food—the water appears deep blue.

Plankton brighten coral reefs

Zooxanthellae, the phytoplankton that live inside coral animals, are temperamental. If the water gets too hot, too cold, or too polluted, they scram, leaving the coral as white as a skeleton.

A coral reef is like a city beneath the sea—busy, crowded, and colorful, just like a metropolis on land. The builders of these vast underwater cities are a type of phytoplankton called *zooxanthellae* and small, vase-shaped animals called coral polyps. Zooxanthellae live inside a thin layer of tissue linking all the coral polyps together.

Zooxanthellae help the coral animals take minerals from the seawater to build their limestone skeletons. They also give the corals their vibrant colors of pink, yellow, orange, purple, or red.

If water conditions get too stressful—too hot, too cold, too polluted—the zooxanthellae may leave or die. Without them, the coral becomes as white as a skeleton. This coral bleaching is being found in more reefs around the globe.

Plankton help invent new products

About eight million tons of plastic are washed into the ocean each year. We know that plastic balloons can be swallowed by seabirds, sea turtles, and seals, choking them. But discarded plastics also can impact the smallest marine animals.

A lot of the plastics that end up in the ocean are less than 1/16 of an inch long (5 millimeters). They are called **microplastics**. Microplastics can be beads, string, or pieces of larger plastics that have broken down into tiny pieces that are nearly invisible. Unfortunately, they are the same size as the plankton that larval clams, krill, and copepods should be eating.

When zooplankton eat microplastics instead of plankton, it can prevent them from being able to swallow their real food. Harmful pollutants adhere to these tiny particles, making these plastic particles even more toxic to marine life.

But scientists are looking for alternatives to plastics. Did you know that seaweeds can replace the plastics that are normally used to make everyday products such as flip flops, surfboards, and straws?

The National Center for Marine Algae and Microbiota inside the Bigelow Laboratory for Ocean Sciences grows more than 2,500 different kinds of phytoplankton and 1,300 different kinds of seaweed. These marine plants are used in global ocean research, to study evolution in plants, and to develop new products, such as **biofuels**, human foods, medicines, hand creams, natural pet foods, and products that can replace plastic.

Threats to Our Superheroes

Warming seas

Climate scientists agree that our planet is warming and that human activity is the primary cause. We are feeling the effects of excess carbon dioxide from smokestacks and tailpipes and other greenhouse gases that trap the heat they produce in the upper atmosphere.

The result—climate change—is warming the oceans, eroding beaches, and disrupting ocean currents around the globe.

We have already warmed the atmosphere by about 1.5 degrees Fahrenheit. As air warms, so does water—by a lot.

Fortunately for those of us who live on land, the ocean has absorbed over 90 percent of the excess heat that we have put into the atmosphere over the last 30 years. Scientists say that if all that heat had gone into the lower atmosphere, the air temperature would be 20 degrees Fahrenheit hotter than it is now!

The ocean is taking one for the team, so to speak, slowing climate change for those of us who live on land. But at what cost to the ocean?

Fractured food web

Rising water temperatures and new predators invading from warmer regions are affecting the food supply of many sea creatures. They are displacing phytoplankton such as diatoms and zooplankton such as copepods, which are rich in fats necessary to sustain the sea creatures that eat them.

Conditions in the ocean are changing. Populations of copepods seem to be declining where ocean waters are warming. That could spell trouble for the entire ocean food web.

As the ocean food web changes, some sea creatures may move, change their diet, or die out altogether. If copepods move, then some of the animals that depend on them, such as lobsters, may move to cooler waters, too.

If creatures have to change their diet, their new food supply might not be as wholesome. Salps thrive in warm water where there is little oxygen. These gelatinous animals are mostly water. They offer very little food value, especially compared to copepods, which can have up to 60 to 70 percent body fat. It's like switching from healthy meals to junk food.

Ocean acidification

The ocean absorbs between 25 and 40 percent of *all* the carbon dioxide that goes into the atmosphere each year from burning fossil fuels, cutting down forests, and other human actions.

A lesser-known consequence of climate change is **ocean acidification**. When water and carbon dioxide mix, they form a weak acid, called *carbonic acid*. It's the same chemical found in carbonated beverages like cola and ginger ale. The fizz that tickles your nose when you open a bottle of soda is carbon dioxide gas escaping. Sadly, carbonic acid can also make sea shells dissolve.

Scientists studying the Pacific Ocean along the west coast of the United States are finding the delicate shells of pteropods pockmarked with holes from swimming in acidic water. Some are dissolving altogether. Scientists worry that with the ocean becoming more acidic, all sea butterflies could be gone by the end of this century.

Shellfish are harmed, too. Baby oysters, mussels, clams, and scallops can suffer the same fate—becoming pitted with tiny holes or even dissolving if the water is too acidic.

0.2 mm

Scientists have discovered that ocean acidification affects many sea creatures with shells, including sea butterflies and coccoliths. The shells of baby clams like this one can become pitted by acidic seawater in just two weeks.

It will take a team of superheroes to save the ocean universe

Where do we start? First, we need to know more about what is happening in the 320 million cubic miles (1.335 billion cubic kilometers) that make up the world ocean.

What is there left to learn? Almost everything.

Scientists and engineers, aided by students and volunteer citizen scientists, are working hard to try to understand what is going on beneath the surface of the ocean. Using microscopes, miniature submarines, research ships, satellites, and even smart phones, they scour the ocean planet to discover the secrets of the global ocean.

With emerging technologies, they are able to look deeper and smaller.

Marine Scientists

Marine scientists, in labs and on ships, are studying the tiniest organisms in the sea. Aided by satellites 440 miles above the earth, they are monitoring how climate change is impacting the ocean even as they are trying to learn what lives there.

Researchers like those at Bigelow Laboratory for Ocean Sciences in Maine examine still unnamed species of plankton, test new technologies, and concoct experiments. Self-guiding submarines travel thousands of miles across the ocean to hunt for plankton before turning around and coming home again. A 48-foot-long research vessel takes scientists around the world to study plankton in cold waters, tropical seas, and the open ocean.

Citizen Scientists

Scientists can't be everywhere to collect the data they need to understand what is happening in and along the ocean. Luckily, they have many helpers in trained volunteers.

These citizen scientists assist researchers in looking for harmful phytoplankton blooms. They are partners in an early-warning system screening coastal waters for red tides.

Volunteers test the health of sea water at swimming beaches. They can detect pollution from stormwater runoff or a sewage spill to warn beachgoers not to go swimming until the water quality improves.

Other volunteers use their smart phones to take photos of coastal flooding caused by extreme high tides and storm surges, dangerous waves that are pushed onshore by wind and rain. They are documenting the effects of sea level rise and coastal erosion in real time.

Some coast watchers use binoculars to record the return of whales to their nearshore feeding grounds each year.

Everything that walks, crawls, or swims—from bacteria to whales—sheds traces of its DNA, which can reveal its genetic makeup. A futuristic research tool can track elusive animals in the jungle that humans rarely get to see, as well as criminals who have left their DNA at a crime scene. It's called Environmental DNA or eDNA.

Think of what scientists—and volunteers—could learn from a jar of seawater. All they need is a smart phone linked to a handheld eDNA monitor. By aiming their cell phone at the jar of water, they can instantly detect the eDNA of red tide phytoplankton—or migrating salmon, endangered whales, even a great white shark that may have been swimming in those waters recently.

We are all the guardians of the ocean

A 24-foot-long North Atlantic right whale, surrounded by supersized plankton, has greeted visitors as they entered the lobby of Bigelow Laboratory for Ocean Sciences. The giant sculpture was created by artists and volunteers using wood scraps, vines, and debris that washed up on local beaches.

It's a reminder that humans, plankton, and all marine life share one world. What we do on land impacts everything that lives in the other 70 percent of the globe, our oceans.

It's a reminder that there is a lot that we can do to protect the ocean. We can:

- Walk or bike instead of asking for a ride.

- Carpool or take public transportation.

- Shop with reusable food storage bags. Whenever possible, use reusable utensils, straws, water bottles, and other containers.

- Many clothes that are made from plastics, such as fleece jackets, shed microplastic fibers when washed. Try to use natural fibers like cotton and wool instead. Or simply don't wash your fleece!

- Help with beach cleanups and park pickups. Make it a habit to pick up trash whenever you're out for a walk.

- When you walk your dog, bag your pet poop and dispose of it in the trash or the toilet.

- Look for programs at your library or community education center that feature new discoveries in science and the environment.

- Do STEM! The ocean needs more people who do Science, Technology, Engineering, and Mathematics!

Glossary

albedo: a measure of the amount of sunlight an object reflects

biofuels: fuels that are derived from renewable sources, such as plants, algae, or animal waste

bioluminescence: the production of light by living things, such as bacteria, phytoplankton, krill, and many other animals, through a chemical reaction

chlorophyll: a chemical in phytoplankton and other plants that helps capture light energy and changes it into chemical energy

coccolithophore: a tiny phytoplankter covered by plates made of calcium carbonate

copepod: a very small, shrimplike zooplankter that is a key animal in the ocean food chain

diatom: a phytoplankter with a glass shell made of silica

dinoflagellate: a phytoplankter that often has two flagella, or tails

food web: a complex interrelationship of who eats whom

harmful algal bloom: a large bloom of toxic or harmful algae; often called red tide

krill: a shrimplike animal that is essential food for many animals

larval: the early stage of an animal between hatching and adulthood

microplastics: plastics less than 1/16 of an inch long (5 millimeters). They can be beads, string, or pieces of larger plastics

nanoplankton: particularly small phytoplankton with sizes between 2 and 20 μm.

nutrients: simple chemicals required for plants and animals to grow and thrive

ocean acidification: the result of when water and carbon dioxide mix, forming a weak acid, called carbonic acid

phytoplankton: plant plankton, which harness the energy of the sun to make their own food; one-celled, microscopic drifting plants; microalgae (singular: phytoplankter)

photosynthesis: process in which light energy from the sun is converted into chemical energy by plants using water and carbon dioxide, resulting in the production of oxygen, sugars, and starches

picoplankton: the smallest phytoplankton, which measure less than 2 micrometers

pteropod: a marine snail whose feet are modified into wings; sea butterfly

salp: a barrel-shaped, gelatinous sea creature

zooplankton: animal plankton that feed on phytoplankton or other zooplankton (singular: zooplankter)

zoop poop: fecal pellets, waste product excreted by a small sea creature

Bibliography

Bang, Molly and Penny Chisholm, *Ocean Sunlight: How Tiny Plants Feed the Seas*, 2012, The Blue Sky Press

Cerullo, Mary, *Life Under Ice*, 2019, Tilbury House

Cerullo, Mary and Beth Simmons, *Sea Secrets: Tiny Clues to a Big Mystery*, 2008, Moonlight Publishing

Lilley, Matt, *Good Eating: The Short Life of Krill*, 2022, Tilbury House

Nicol, Stephen, *The Curious Life of Krill: A Conservation Story from the Bottom of the World*, 2018, Island Press

Library of Congress Cataloging-in-Publication Data

Names: Cerullo, Mary M., author.
Title: Tiny titans : the big story of plankton / Mary M. Cerullo.
Description: [Ann Arbor, Michigan] : [Tilbury House Publishers], [2024] |
Series: How nature works | Audience: Ages 7-12 | Summary: "Discover the enormous world of some of the planet's tiniest creatures-and the giant job they do in our ecosystem. From zooplankton to phytoplankton, these small-scale superheroes are the foundation of the ocean's food chain, keep our climate in check, generate oxygen-and much more"-- Provided by publisher.
Identifiers: LCCN 2024011326 | ISBN 9781668944844 (hardcover)
Subjects: LCSH: Plankton--Juvenile literature.
Classification: LCC QH90.8.P5 C47 2024 | DDC 578.77/6--dc23/eng/20240416
LC record available at https://lccn.loc.gov/2024011326

TILBURY HOUSE PUBLISHERS™

an imprint of Cherry Lake Publishing Group
2395 South Huron Parkway, Suite 200
Ann Arbor, MI 48104
www.tilburyhouse.com

Printed and bound in the United States

10 9 8 7 6 5 4 3 2 1

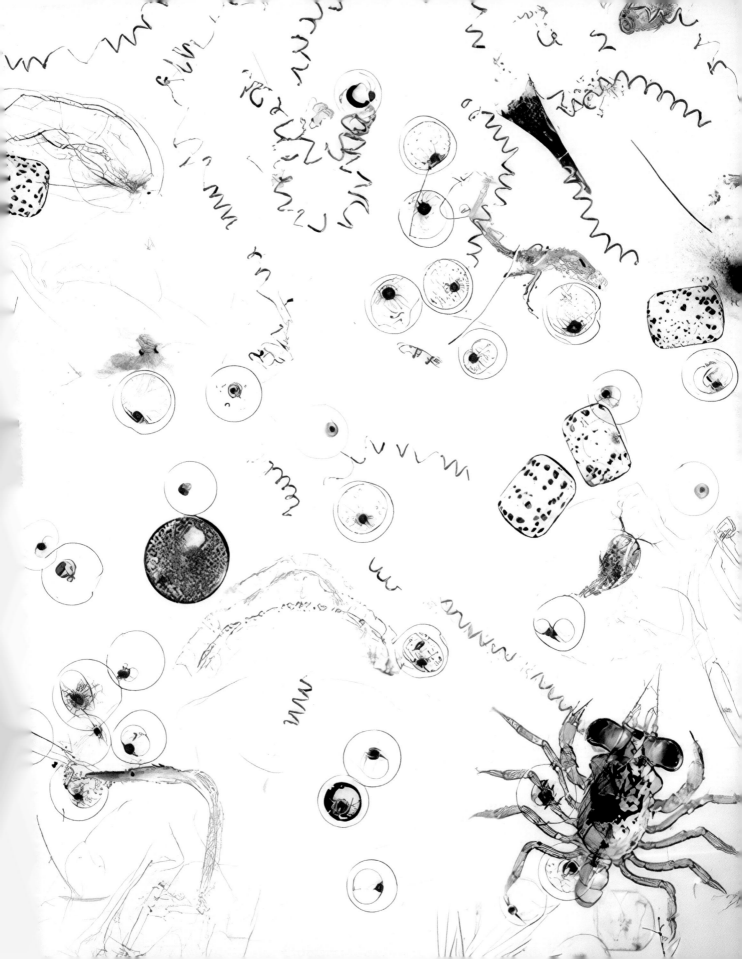

Acknowledgments

Many thanks to the staff of Bigelow Laboratory for Ocean Sciences, East Boothbay, Maine: Steven Profaizer, Chief Communications Officer, Michael Lomas, PhD, National Center for Marine Algae and Microbiota, Laura Lubelczyk, and Peter Countway, PhD.

Special thanks go to Leah Campbell, Science Communications Manager, who researched photographs from Bigelow's collection for this book, and most especially to Nick Record, PhD, Senior Research Scientist, Tandy Center for Ocean Forecasting Director, who advised and assisted me throughout the research and writing process, from initial ideas to finished product. Any errors are my own.

The whale installation on p. 54-55 was created by Sculptor Andy Rosen and his assistant David Mahany and coordinated by artist Anna Dibble, in conjunction with Gulf of Maine EcoArts. This Maine artists' collaborative also organized and built "Sea Change: Darkness & Light in the Gulf of Maine" at the Maine Maritime Museum—where the whale was featured a second time. The whale was then moved to the arts and education center at Wabanaki Public Health & Wellness in Bangor, Maine.

Dedication

To Arthur, my biggest cheerleader for 50 years and counting

About the Author

Mary M. Cerullo describes herself as a science interpreter, using her skills as a teacher and a writer to make research understandable to non-scientists. Mary is the award-winning author of 24 children's books on the ocean, from phytoplankton to great white sharks.